Gr

To my husband, who ~~is my~~ sounding board, my encourager, my life partner, my assigned person and the reason I chose this topic. I truly realized how much I needed you. Infidelity was a sting, yes heart drenching, but your repentance showed up in your constant love and consistency. The Bible states that love hides a multitude of sin. I forgave you wholeheartedly and chose to continue our marriage walking in God's unconditional love. Our latter is truly greater. I will love you forever Dear!

My daughter Raven, who is a two time published author, invited me to attend author school with her. My first response was absolutely not. I had already managed elementary, high school, business school and went on to completing graduate school. I was done with school, or so I thought.

The morning of the final day of registration the Spirit prompted me to register and I obeyed. It was the beginning of my journey to becoming a published author. I'm forever grateful to her for the invite powered by God. She and I walked blindly hand and hand through Author School, trusting God to take us to its completion, as He did.

In order to write the book, I had to revisit the betrayal. This is where my eldest daughter, Zarie stepped in. She provided mental and emotional support. She was my cheerleader, encouraging me to hang in there. We spent hours on the phone. I didn't want to be a forunner as a healed betrayed wife. I didn't choose this for myself. Yet, I embraced the call to model God's forgiveness and unconditional love in a tight spot.

"This book will help other women who are struggling to overcome infidelity," Zarie said. "They will come to understand choosing purpose over pain."

She listened and gave feedback as I penned my healed heart on paper. I say healed heart because God allowed me to recognize and accept that I had walked through this entire ordeal with Him there all the time. It was for the purpose and not the pain.

Lastly, to my sunshine (Barbara Ann Esteen) gone but never forgotten. She was my support system, my listening hear, my confidant. She loved like the big sister that every girl would want in thier life. I can hear you now "Save your energy pudding. Put it in a damn book. It's called LIFEing."

I love you Barb and I put it in the damn book!

Introduction..Blah Blah Blah!!

What if we acknowledge daily that In order to WIN in our marriage it is imperative that we let go and trust God. Transform our mind to think like Jesus. We must choose Purpose over Pain!

What if simply shifting our patterns of thinking could really change our marriage life? A change that would allow us to test and approve what God's good and perfect will is for marriages. We know that we live in an imperfect world, but we still serve a perfect God.

Can we agree that mind transformation is absolutely necessary? We make this shift in our thinking to allow God to do His perfect will in our marriage. "Resist conformity to the thoughts and actions of this world," and conform to HIS divine order.

Forward

My book journey forced me to revisit hurts and disappointments of my past. I had to, for the second time, face the pain and disappointments that lead me to this journey.

Writing this book has been healing from the inside out. I was challenged to love out loud, despite the unsolicited voices that carried my dead issues of marriage.

This journey has been both anxious and exciting. Anxious, because of my own insecurities and exciting because I get to share how God turned my pain into purpose.

Note: When people bring things up from your past, let it remind you of your victory, even if you feel you aren't there yet. Most importantly, remember that you have matured and grown spiritually. Be reminded of how happy you are that you've moved from where those voices reside. Realize that only those who truly understand God's purpose in marriage can walk with you in this season.

Many of us google everything (directions/instructions, advice to find an answer/solution, etc.). What if we learned to work scripture like we work hard at learning our new air fryer, new car, new electronic device (cell phone, tablet, smart TV)?

Finally, do we treat biblical solutions that can save our marriages with the blah blah blah response?!

Right about now is when we declare not another scorning of scriptures.

I need some solutions to help alleviate the headaches, pain and disappointments from this husband.

The husband that I am ready to throw away!! I'm tired and ready to throw in the towel… and I definitely can't comprehend my latter being greater. In fact, I am not sure if there is help for this marriage. He has crossed the line. I want out! I don't want to partner with him anymore!!

Table of Contents

Chapter 1 ……Bitter Disappointment

Chapter 2…… Revisiting Joy & Pain

Chapter 3…… Wearing A Mask

Chapter 4…… Struggling To Forgive

Chapter 5…….Trust Issues

Chapter 6……. Choosing Purpose

Chapter 7……. Surviving Infidelity

Chapter 8……I'm Keeping My Husband

Chapter 1
Bitter Disappointment

Throw the whole husband away! Father God aint nobody got TIME for this. I don't want this husband anymore. As a person challenged with anxiety much of my adult life......I've already been in a battle with time. If outcomes take too long for me, it's a problem! I didn't know that I was about to be stung by a pain and disappointment that would break me into pieces. Pieces that God would strategically and divinely put back together again. Time didn't seem to be on my side.

Things had taken a wide turn in our marriage. Intimacy had escaped. Conversations were minimum and asking questions were inappropriate. I didn't like being hugged up, but I loved his hugs. Intimacy became a one-sided thing. Even me reaching out for a hug had become a problem. Usually I could fall in his chest and wrap myself around him at pleasure. He would jokingly say " What do you want now dear?". My reply was always, "You." I just want a bear hug. After a while he started folding up, appearing to be busy or in a rush. I'm not the one to plead, but I found myself asking for hugs. I would wave and tease "Hey dear, Are you forgetting something? What about me?" He would never leave the house without a goodbye.

However, a couple of times I made my way to the door and he was already pulling off or gone. No hugs, no kiss or goodbye. He was rushing off to work. He was rushing off to church or somewhere unknown to me. Thoughts of him cheating was definitely not my "first" thought. He worked two jobs and was active daily in ministry. Maybe he's exhausted and overworked I would think.

He was preoccupied. Me reminding him of our daily routines (hug, kiss and goodbye) irritated him. He even reminded me that he was not the hugging kind. He didn't like it. At least that's what he said. He started giving me short answers to my questions. My questions were valid. We had daily rituals that were slowly disappearing. His answers were short and at times abrupt. I would ask, where are you going now? You just got home. This never phased him before. Our norm when leaving the house was a hug, I love you and I'll be back. He began saying "What's with all the questions?" He even mentioned to me that I may want to find something to do with my time. He said that I seemed to be bored. This was strange coming from him. He wanted me at home.

He said that I should be there when the kids got in from school or when he got off from work.
What had happened to him? Where was this coming from. He seemed so distant. What is happening to us? How did we get here? Did I do or say something wrong?

You backtrack the years of happiness looking for any possible situation, issues or occurrences that could have transpired between the two of you. What could have angered him? Why am I being ignored? Why are there so many complaints? You tip top around the discontentment displayed by your spouse. You timidly question his anger and new behaviors that he is displaying. Each time the two of you face a new situation or disagreement you take responsibility to avoid conflict. Also, to avoid being shut out even more. It becomes obvious and overwhelming that your partner has zoned out of this partnership. You're trying to process the change and fully acknowledge that there is a change.

As you struggle to walk in the presence of a preoccupied spouse, you approach him again with caution. This time with intentional caution; almost as if he is the victim. You need answers as to why there is so much distance and discontentment. Surely he could talk to me about whatever was concerning him. You can't put your hands on the reason. The reason your spouse is so preoccupied. Your prayers changes drastically from God whatever this is, I know you can work it out...to, I need to know!

Suddenly my thoughts changed. I begin to consider the possibility of cheating. You begin to petition God! Lord your word says in Luke chapter 12, "There is nothing concealed that will not be disclosed, or hidden that will not be made known. What you have said in the dark will be heard in the daylight, and what you have whispered in the ear in the inner rooms will be proclaimed from the roofs." God I need to know. I need you to reveal the truth!

Then there is that fear of the unknown. Do you really want to know? With Your heart racing and thoughts rambling you switch to I don't want to know. I trust you God to fix it.

You are disappointed that you feel so disappointed. Why are my expectations so high? Men will be men. Mad, Because you're walking in innocence. You've done nothing to provoke anyone.

Angrier!!, that someone is consuming your peaceful space! You're thinking, if he's unhappy here he should leave. You're fearful for you and the children. Your peaceful sanctuary has been invaded with toxic energy. His speech is not lining up with his actions.

This was most difficult.

He always had a lot to say. I often sat quietly. He did all the talking. He even answered folks when they were talking to or questioning me. I hadn't realized how voiceless I was. And now to confront him seemed disrespectful. It doesn't take a rocket scientist to gure out some obvious things. I was naïve, but not to the point of cluelessness. Maybe I was!

This was a long hard journey for me. I was a stay at home mom. The world outside of my home was ever evolving. My husband stayed current and in the know. It was church, Walmart and home for me. Unless we took a mini vacation as we often did. My children were young and I depended on him heavily. Communication was a necessity in our day to day lives. We were raising ten children. He had become unavailable daily. I was forced to make daily decisions without his approval. This was denitely a new thing. I was somewhat intimidated by his aggression. He was a control freak. And to be honest, I didn't mind it. Baring the children and guiding the house of twelve was enough.

Nevertheless, I managed.

Days turned into weeks and weeks turned in to months. It seems hopeless. Nothing could have prepared me for the reveal. A reveal that would send someone immediately into a panic attack! Well I mean that's where it sent me. It made sense to think that he was just exhausted with having to carry such a hugh load. Working two jobs to provide for a family of twelve and full time ministry.

Whether it has already been revealed, or you are waiting for answers to the blank spots, I pray your strength in God. I pray right now that God's peace will surround you. I pray that He will cover you and your children if there be children. I'm trusting that He turns your tears and mourning into laughter. Most of all, I pray that you will continue to trust and believe that God is still on the throne. I give you a glimpse of hope.... God is not in the business of failure. He NEVER fails!!

"There is nothing concealed that will not be disclosed, or hidden that will not be made known. What you have said in the dark will be heard in the daylight, and what you have whispered in the ear in the inner rooms will be proclaimed from the roofs.
Luke 12: 2-3 NIV

The Reveal

Well, let me race forward with the uncovering of this mystery. I was becoming bitter by the day. Imagine someone telling you how important you are but treating you as irrelevant. A sudden shift from being treated as an amazing wife to a nanny and caregiver. Something was going on. I was in the mist of something intangible.

I walked right upon it. The heart drenching reveal. The answer to his madness. The answer that kept him preoccupied. The thing that turned his eyes away from me.

I was preparing a lesson for an upcoming Women's ministry event and I could not nd the binder that I kept my materials in. I needed it. I searched everywhere and then it dawned on me that it was left in my husband's vehicle. Church being ten minutes away, I took a quick run to the church to retrieve it from his vehicle.

He worked the night shift. Every morning after work, he drove to church to facilitate a car wash. I pulled up in the church's parking lot next to his truck. I jumped out and proceeded to open the door. When I opened the door, immediately staring me in the face was a white envelope on the console leaning against the side of the driver's seat. It was neatly sealed. Written in capital letters was the word "LADY". It bared his familiar handwriting on the outside. Startled, I stared initially while questions swapped my brain. Moving in trance like motion, a flood of emotions encompassed me. The name on the envelope confirmed that it was not written for me.

I hesitated to reach for it. Then suddenly, I could not remember why I was in my husband's vehicle. Still, my eyes were fixed on the envelope.

The envelope that paralyzed my thoughts and made my memory cloudier. The word "LADY", that instantly killed my spirit.

Was this the secret? The REVEAL? The uncovering of the mystery that held my bleeding heart in bondage. Did God answer my prayer? Tears began to well up in my eyes. Shaking, I picked up the envelope, dropped to the passenger seat and sat still. Suddenly the door opened. It was my hubby, my friend, my lover, my life partner.

His face wore a look of urgency and disbelief. He hurried into the driver's seat and immediately began explaining or trying to tell me how he wanted to surprise me with a "just because." In the mist of his weak explanation, he reached toward me for the envelope. I pulled back. I whispered "for me right?" He replied, " yes dear." I muffled up enough voice to say "LADY?", but I'm Dear remember. The name he affectionately called me.

He stared in shock and sat in stillness.

I forcefully exited his vehicle.

I jumped in my car with my thoughts still cloudy. My heart was palpitating to an unknown rhyme. My eyes were filled with emotions and my stomach was uttering. I drove home, clinging to the envelope. I was contemplating setting it on fire, so maybe I would forget this happened and remember it no more. But, if you've been there you already know the curiosity was driving me insane. I had one panic attack after another. The ten minute drive seemed like forever. Finally, I pulled in my driveway, sat quietly in my car and opened the mysterious envelope. The tears blurred my vision whereas I had to start reading it over and over again. As soon as I began reading, I burst into tears! The reading. The wording. The signature!

I don't have to tell you... if this has happened to you, then you already know what it was like when you stared face to face with truth. No more questions of what's wrong with him or what have I done. It's now a host of new questions. How long has this been going on? When did it happen? Where did it take place? Why didn't I see it coming? Who is LADY?!

I trained myself to believe he was so caught up in ministry that he ignored us. I even said to myself...He's doing God's business. God's business comes first. I guess I denounced us as a part of God's business. You know how we can sometimes blame people's behavior on ministry and not the person. We know as Christian's that the Bible declares in Romans 14:12. "So then, each of us will give an account of ourselves to God."

> *So then, each of us will give an account of ourselves to God*
>
> *Romans 14:12*

It's early morning and I'm already exhausted! I exit the car and drag myself inside our used to be or so I thought, or maybe it was, or maybe it still can be.. happy home. We woman of God know how to pre-occupy ourselves with busy hideaway work. Nothing was working for me. I knew he would return home early, but not too early.

Maybe 45 minutes to the hour after my arrival home I heard his key turn the door open.

He rushed towards me. I pushed him away. He bear held me again without a release and I wept and wept uncontrollably. He would not let me go. He begin to tell me how desperately he wanted to end it. You know the thing that he was caught up in. I pushed back, pounding his chest, screaming...

"Why? WHY? How could you do this to us. How could you just throw away all the love we shared. This is not who you are. What a fool I was. I loved you with everything inside of me. I honored and respected you as a powerful man of God. How could you be such a disappointment?"

My scattered thoughts were raging. You know, that feeling of thinking and believing with everything inside of you that your marriage was solid? I thought we were solid. I said to him, "I thought with all my heart that our marriage was solid." His response angered me to my core.
"We are 'DEAR' we are solid!"
"Don't call me that," I screamed! "I'm not your dear. I can't be."
" It's not what you are thinking," he shouted, as if I were delusional. With my heart broken into a billion pieces; I asked again, "Who is she? Who is lady and why did you sign Loving...", I could not get the other words out.
Never mind, I don't wanna know. Who is she? How long? Why? Needless to say, time did not seem to be on my side. I wanted him gone, thrown away like trash. I didn't want him anymore. It made me feel sick to look at him. Did God forget what I said? Infidelity was definitely a divorce for me.
Let's just say he called her a "Billie Jean"... not his lover. I just got caught up he said. She's nobody dear. I'm sorry. I love you. I love my family. This is not who I am.
How do you push forward with the news, the tragedy, disloyalty and the REVEAL of spousal betrayal?

Chapter 2
Revisiting Joy And Pain

To say I was angry is an understatement. I don't know about you, but the betrayal was devastating. A devastation that overwhelms you. A hurt that overtakes your entire being. It's hard to focus. You question God's presence.

Have you ever experienced a hard hit in your life's journey? One that left you distorted. A hit that thrust you to silence! Fighting to win turned to a fight to vanish! In the midnight hours, your sorrows leak onto your pillow. You lay motionless in the mist of betrayal!

You yearn for your life to return to the blissful state that the two of you once shared. The long rides to the country. The kids loved going to their grandparents (Big Mama and Bubba) house in Manseld, LA, Highway 84. Their dad would stop on the side of the road and let them pick cotton. I guess you are wondering why would he want them to pick cotton. It was a history lesson. The kids had never touched real cotton in a cotton field.

He shared his grandmother's days of picking cotton. She would pull a sack of cotton while pulling him on an empty sack tied to her waist. She would pick one row and swing the bag to the next row. He would ride the sack watching the workers swiftly pick cotton. He said big mama would be drenched in sweat dragging him and the cotton. He called that a lot of love. I called it abuse.

The boys loved playing in the backyard pond. Big Mama would make time to play with them, while Bubba would take them in the chicken coup to collect eggs. He would let them walk the corn field with him. The boys would help gather logs for the fireplace. The girls would sing gospel songs for Big Mama. The songs they sang in church choir. She would tear up, clapping and smiling. Hubby would take the kids out in the field and give them shooting lessons. He would set up empty cans as targets. I hated it, but the kids loved it.

They had horses, cows, hogs, geese, chickens, roosters, dogs and cats. They even had pet raccoons on the farm. Our city kids embraced country life with much excitement. I loved the sound of crickets. I couldn't wait to hear the loud sounds at night. My love would collect crickets in a jar. He would put holes in the top of the jar and bring them to me.

I would sit on the front porch with Big Mama and admire the beauty of nature. I loved waking up to the sound of roosters crowing. The kids and I were in country heaven. The "bestest " as they would call it, was riding the go cart up and down the hills with their cousins. The younger children were intrigued with the tree house. Their cousins would take them one by one up the ladder to the treehouse. It was the best experience of country living.

We took the kids to the beach often. We would fake bury the kids in the sand. Then we would fake bury dad in the sand. The kids would throw sand in dad's eyes and hair. They had him spitting out sand. The funny part is when they started fake burying me. The kids would carefully throw in sand to cover my body. When the sand got too high or close to my face, they would shout "that's enough dad." That melted my heart. We would spend a day at the beach and a day canoeing at Blackwater Rivers.

There was this one time we were canoeing and the water was very shallow. The canoe 2 of my teenage daughters were in tipped over. One of my daughters was rolling around in the water screaming bloody murder. Her father yelled from our canoe "stand up" but she continued to fight the water. He then got out of the canoe, went to her, and stood her up. "Calm down." he said. "Look the water is at your knees."

Her teary eyes looked around and realized she was standing. We all began to laugh hysterically. She then joined in with giggles. Boy what a wonderful time it was.

So many fun memories. We had so much fun. We were the Hodges' Bunch! There was so much love between us. There were movie nights and karaoke. I wasn't a movie lover, but my hubby was. He and the kids would go to blockbusters and rent movies. They would return home and watch movies back to back. I was often bored with movies, but I loved karaoke night. I tried singing gospel songs during karaoke, but they said I sound as if I was singing the blues. It was the blues alright, then Gospel music lol.

The best karaoke performances were at Christmas. My husband facilitated karaoke performances. He was super serious about the competitions. Whoever stopped by our house Christmas day, had to participate. when he handed you the mic you had to say something. "Just introduce yourself and your family," he would say. He handed out cash prizes for the winners. There was always a first, second and third place winner. The children participated separately from the adults. Many family and friends would show up at Christmas just to participate in the karaoke contest.

We would line up as many chairs that would fit in the performance area. Some sat two to a chair. It was a big deal! My husband loved celebrating with the kids, family and friends. He would cook a huge breakfast the morning of. Breakfast included grits, eggs, bacon, shrimp, scallops, fish, frog legs, steak, biscuits and french toast. Then, there was his famous fruit tray with watermelon, honeydew melon, cantaloupe, mango, kiwi, grapes, plums or whatever fruit were in season. It was a huge spread. He was the best host ever!!

Then there was Tuesday family night at Ryan steakhouse. We would pack our 15 passenger van with our children, neighborhood children, other moms and their kids. It was another means of ministry.

So many beautiful memories flooded my mind. Then suddenly, I would drift off to overthinking. You know when you start overthinking and over analyzing your state of being. You're remembering the beautiful life you shared. Yet, over and over you try to picture her. You know, Lady. What did she do to draw him so close? You try to remember the nights you could have possibly pushed him away.

Your mind is at war. You are trying to preserve the beauty and process the ashes simultaneously. There's no way this is happening. We were so in love. He cherished me. He showed up for our family. He spoke so highly of me as referring to a Proverbs 31 woman.

> 28 Her children arise and call her blessed; her husband also, and he praises her: 29 "Many women do noble things, but you surpass them all." 30 Charm is deceptive, and beauty is fleeting; but a woman who fears the LORD is to be praised.
> Proverbs 31: 28-30

If I said I wanted a piece of the sky, he would try and make it happen. We had one car and he would leave the car with me and the kids and ride a bike to work. He was overprotective of us. He provided us (me and the ten kids) with everything we needed. He tried his best to give us the things we wanted too. He often neglected himself so sacrificially.

There is no way he didn't love us. He wasn't much on communicating his love verbally. He often called that sort of communication mushy talk "player lines." Maybe the player lines he used on 'LADY". At least that is what I chose to believe. He didn't just talk about loving us, he showed us how much he loved us. I called him my man of action! We could always count on him. There's no way he would consciously hurt us. There's no way he would consciously betray us, well me. He said many women did noble things, but I surpassed them all. He loved me into believing that he loved me...if that makes sense. He was always available for us.

Why question someone who gave so selflessly?

You begin to share blame for his behaviors. What did I do? Thinking maybe you were too busy attending to the kids. Maybe it was the nights you were so exhausted you fell asleep. Maybe you had become too passive or boring. So many thoughts that would have tied knots in your brain. Lying there, I prayed and wept to be rocked in the bosom of the almighty God. The all knowing God. It's no way he doesn't know that this is happening to us. God sees it all. He is here with us. He said in His word that He would **NEVER** leave or forsake us. I believed just what He said.

Then, there's that flood of uncontrollable emotions. Your mental emotions triggers choking and coughing as that of an acute exacerbation attack. You smother your cries, so as not to fall in ear range of your sleeping children.

After which you lay in silence. When you return from your subconscious state, you realize that you had fallen asleep. You look around as one held hostage in a foreign country. You wept during the night, but there was no joy in the morning.
God where are you now?

When I came to myself I began to pray for me and other wounded women all over the world. Women who shared the same pain and disappointment or similar. With the little strength you have, you try to pull yourself together. You hope and pray for the dawn of a new day! In spite of the trials and tribulations we as women of God go through, we manage to give thanks to God for another day, Another chance and another opportunity. We are always hoping for the best.

This was a very dark season of marriage. Was I the only one who felt like "TIME" was moving in slow motion?

Did you wrestle with determining how to show up daily? What mask to wear? Did you question your ability to forgive and move on?

I was so angry, but I was struggling to walk in my purpose. God had called and ordained me with purpose. Nothing would be able to separate me from the love of God, which is in Christ Jesus. Yes, Nothing!! I read devotion after devotion. Whatever the disappointment.....continue to hold fast to God's word. The devotional on the following pages gave me a little breakthrough.

Casting Doubts Aside

The speaker in today's Scripture reading gains a new perspective on his suffering when he thinks on God's faithfulness.

> "I have been deprived of peace; I have forgotten what prosperity is. So I say, "My splendor is gone and all that I had hoped from the Lord." I remember my affliction and my wandering, the bitterness and the gall. Yet this I call to mind and therefore I have hope: They are new every morning; great is your faithfulness. I say to myself, "The Lord is my portion; therefore I will wait for him." Lamentations 3:17-24

Pray
God, I am struggling to have hope that you are working in my favor. Teach me to trust your love for me and your faithfulness, even when my circumstances suggest otherwise.

Read
The speaker in today's Scripture reading gains a new perspective on his suffering when he thinks on God's faithfulness.

Reflect

What does the speaker remember? He calls to mind that the love of God is unceasing, his kindness is dependable, and "the Lord can always be trusted to show mercy each morning" (v. 23 CEV). Despite all the things that made him feel hopeless, despaired, and insecure about his future, this moment of reflection centers him—it brings him back to truths about God that give him confidence that better things are ahead.

Respond

Let John Newton's 1779 hymn "Amazing Grace" ll your heart with hope that God is faithful and will see you through your hardships. Let it relinquish your doubts and build your condence in God who will lead you all the way.
http://bibleresources.americanbible.org/

I continued to trust God. Well, let's just say, daily I wore a mask.

Chapter 3
Wearing a Mask: Living Life Uncovered

You might notice that developing a habit of hiding painful emotions leads to habitual rage. Jane Collingwood explains in a psych central online article that such a lifestyle of anger destroys relationships and creates bitterness. Have the courage to allow yourself to own the truth of your experience. Otherwise, holding onto hostility can keep you stuck.

You must look the part when the kids come in from school. You dare not show any signs of discombobulation. The kids must be kept in safety. You must keep them out of the know. You switch from sadness to survival mod; the mask. Do it for the children, your inner being whispers. They need you whole, not broken.

I don't know if you had the same experience with your children, but there was always that one kid. The one who senses the change in your repetitious nurturing behavior. They bring on the questions. What's wrong mommy? Why are you crying? Did you hurt yourself? Do you have a bobo? You can't whole back the tears. You began sobbing masked with fabricated stories to protect the innocent. Don't cry mommy! Then comes the hugs you so desperately needed.

I don't know about you, but every time I looked at my babies, I felt a fight and flight in me. A fight to keep my family together. A fight to keep my children in a safe zone. Believe it or not, a ght to cover my husband.

Then there was the flight to abandon the marriage. The anger masked hurt was smothering me. Every time I tried to push forward, the voices in my head sped up. Even when I didn't feel so angry, I thought I should be. As Paul stated in Romans 7:19 and 25 " for the good that I would I do not: but the evil which I would not, that I do. For in my inner being I delight in God's law, vs 25.

The virtuous woman that I lived to be was warring with the old soul who secretly wanted revenge. As if I were hiding my feelings from God. I hid behind a mask to survive. Vulnerable emotions beneath the bluster and rage. It wasn't until later in life that I realized that I was hidden in the secret of His tabernacle.

> For I do not do the good I want to do, but the evil I do not want to do—this I keep on doing
> Romans 7:19

> Thanks be to God, who delivers me through Jesus Christ our Lord! So then, I myself in my mind am a slave to God's law, but in my sinful nature[a] a slave to the law of sin
> Romans 7:25

This new season of my life was not welcomed. I didn't care what lesson it was teaching or what I was supposed to be learning. I was bitter and very angry. I showed up daily in disguise. The woman of God and the old soul I used to be were warring. The woman of God was thirsty for healing. The old use to be woman masked in smiles and good deeds was showing up. My flesh wanted revenge. I heard multiple times in my head "vengeance is mine, saith the lord, I will repay." My spirit was willing, but my flesh was weak. I wanted him to feel my wrath.

I had sacrificed my life to be all that he needed me to be. The thought of continuing as a virtuous woman to him felt insane. I said to myself...you (my spouse) are the leader of this marriage. If this (betrayal) is what we are doing, I am here for it. My thoughts, oh God! My every day thoughts were twisted. Maybe I was angrier than disappointed. Because, ALL men cheat right?! That was not surprising! Still, I chose to believe that my man of God was an exemption. Vainly, I thought that he would never betray me. The nerve of him.

Who the hell is Lady?

I was given the topic forgiveness to speak on at a Women's breakfast. I didn't want to show up. Why ask me at a time like this? I prayed at the podium asking God to have His way. Not my will, but His will be done. While teaching, evil thoughts were pressing me. My spirit battling my flesh to dismiss this evil. You don't want to tell other women to forgive the anguish you are currently walking through. I realized my desire to please God was greater than pleasing my flesh. I simply adored being God's vessel. God had been so faithful.

So, with my head up, masked up, I ministered. Dressed in God's armor, I felt protected. Beneath the armor was a wounded soldier. Yet, a soldier familiar with the battlefield. One who had been victorious so many times. As always, God used me in a mighty way. The truth of God's word gave me strength.

In closing, I stated that my forgiveness level was 70 times 7, plus some. For if ye forgive men their trespasses, your heavenly Father will also forgive you. God said it, I believed it and that settles it. God's word was delivered to me first. Hebrews 4:12 states: "For the word of God is quick, and powerful, and sharper than any twoedged sword, piercing even to the dividing asunder of soul and spirit, and of the joints and marrow, and is a discerner of the thoughts and intents of the heart."

> *For the word of God is alive and active. Sharper than any double-edged sword, it penetrates even to dividing soul and spirit, joints and marrow; it judges the thoughts and attitudes of the heart*
> *Hebrews 4:12*

I didn't want to participate in fellowship after the breakfast. The thought of the TALK and fellowship event was mentally draining. I knew it was necessary.

It's time to mask up again: Anger masked hurt! The mental embarrassment I walked through at the end of this powerful/powerless fellowship. Powerful to share God's truth and powerless because I was struggling to forgive. Many women came up to me to tell me how much the message blessed their lives. They would tell me how powerful the message was. They would even make statements like "your husband is blessed to have you." They would pair our names in conversation. "You and your husband" are power houses. Y'all are such a power COUPLE. You guys are awesome role models. I would struggle to stay focussed. Our names mentioned together in the same sentence triggered me. If only they knew!

Walking around wearing a mask was spooky. Whether I was at a church event, in Walmart, or a department store, I felt spooked. I stared at random women wondering if they were Lady. Is she staring at me? Is there a smirk on her face? Does she know who I am? Do I look weak and vulnerable? What a fool I must be?

Unanswered questions lived rent free in my mind. Can they see behind this mask? Who knows my truth? If they only knew how angry I was. Angry toward unknown women. Women I targeted in my mind. My thoughts were drenched in revenge. The mask was still on. Had I really chosen unforgiveness?

Chapter 4

The Struggle To Forgive

I could not believe that I had so easily forgiven him and moved on. I felt healed. I had to stop overthinking and revisiting the issues that broke me to pieces and silenced me. The pain that had me wondering if the entire world was laughing at me. Still wondering Who knew about this? You know "Lady." Have you ever felt like you were the only one in the dark?

We know that the bible says to know no man after the flesh, but by the spirit. We know it says to forgive seventy times seven. I thought, "How many times can a wife forgive this behavior? That is a rhetorical question right, 70 times 7. Can you forgive him and move on without wanting to cause him the same hurt and disappointment? I thought in my heart that I had forgiven him. The Bible states that the heart is deceitful above all things and desperately wicked; who can know it!

A year or two had passed. Things seemed pretty normal. Though I must say that I made some drastic changes. One of the biggest changes was cutting my hair. My hair was one of the things my husband adored. It was long, thick, jet black and luxurious looking. Never in a million years would I have cut my hair. Well, I woke up one Saturday morning with a new attitude. It was a difficult season for me. I called a stylist asking to be a walk- in at the hair salon. Once I arrived there, I almost changed my mind. But, the stylist talked me into a new look. A very short hair style. I wanted to see the look on his face; when he'd realized that the long fluffy, flowing hair that he adored was gone. I wanted him to know that the new hairdo was for me. I had always wanted to cut my hair short. Each time he would talk me out of it. This time it was about me. It was the length and style that I had chosen. After all, my long hair could not have really mattered. The hairstyle he often complimented. The beautiful hair that became invisible to him.

I even changed my wardrobe. I was wearing long shapeless shift dresses as to conceal my body shape. I considered myself as one who wore modest apparell. I didn't want to be stared at or given compliments. I was settled and at peace with who I was. I loved my homely look. The Christian look I thought. I assumed he had become bored with my subtle look. So, I eased into a new look. I added sheath dresses to my wardrobe. I wanted to emphasize the shape of my figure. I thought if I got a new look he would pay more attention to me. I mean, someone would notice me!

Priscilla Shirer is an American author, motivational speaker, actress, and Christian media personality, and evangelist. She stated in her podcast (protecting your spiritual lifeline), that the enemy will keep you paralyzed in your insecurities. She said that he would find the frailty of your mate. The enemy had already found the frailty of my husband. He had already weakened him and led him astray. He knew that my husband had been forgiven by God and focused again. Yet, I was still walking in unforgiveness. The enemy's plan was to hinder the helpmate in this marriage.

The enemy was now setting me up. Blinded by his tactics, as Shirer mentioned you could be using the wrong weapons to win. I know I was. When I walked in the house, he looked shocked, but was silent. After the betrayal, he made less demands. He did not want to do anything to trigger me. I was familiar with him and I was able to recognize the change in his countenance.

His demeanor was different. Although God had forgiven him, he appeared as one walking in shame. I had never seen him that way. He was always confident and in control. A true soldier on the battlefield for God. A man of valor. The man I admired so much. Let me be transparent here. I knew I was part of the reason he was lacking confidence in his leadership. My "don't tell or suggest anything to me" attitude was probing.

To be honest, I needed a change. I needed to become my own person. I needed to find my voice. He had always been the decision maker, the leader. I didn't participate in decision making. I trusted his leadership. I harkened to his voice as the women of the olden days. I had no problem bearing the children and guiding the house. I was satised with mothering my children and catering to my husband. Who can find a virtuous woman? He did. I felt honored to be his wife.

I don't think I ever considered myself as one in need of a separate identity.

Identifying as a woman of God, his wife and the mother of his children seemed to be enough. Maybe I had placed my husband too high on a pedestal! I needed to reposition God. The pedestal was for God and God only! I saw my husband as a man after God's own heart. I relinquished so much power to him. My expectations of him as a man were unattainable.

I remember saying to God, I can walk through anything with my husband except adultery. It didn't matter what the sin was, just don't let it be adultery. I said to God that I would not be able to handle or forgive such a sin. Such a betrayal would destroy me.

The very thought of adultery sickened me.

Thinking of him being intimate with someone else was mind blowing. I mean the same intimacy he shared with me.. I must say, we had some pretty good times. We lived on the wild side a little. Surely he would not share that with another woman. I could never love or trust him again.

Or so I thought.

Studying God's word was so vital to us. My husband often stated that the Bible was man's greatest weapon. He was such a great teacher. One of my favorite bible verses was Psalm 119:11, Thy word have I hid in mine heart, That I might not sin against thee. God had written scriptures on the tables of our hearts that we might not sin against Him. But, was I willing to walk in the Spirit so that I would not fulfill the lust of my flesh.

The attention the new me was getting was welcoming at times. The compliments turned my hubby's head toward the unctuous one. I was attered. The new me would get dolled up wearing lipstick and fashion jewelry. I barely ever wore lipstick. I would head out as if I had someplace to be.

Sort of intentional provoking, right!

> *I have hidden your word in my heart that I might not sin against you*
> *Psalms 119:11*

I was a Bible scholar. I knew God's word. I knew 1 Peter 5:8. Be sober, be vigilant; because your adversary the devil, as a roaring lion, walketh about, seeking whom he may devour. In the midst of my struggle, the enemy allowed me to run across an old friend. An old friend I dated before my husband and I married. It was clearly a platonic relationship, so I thought. What could possibly go wrong with me having lunch with an old friend? Surely it would not go any further. I loved my husband with all my heart. I knew he loved me and was sorry for what he'd done. He was even sorriest that he had sinned against God. He allowed the enemy access to our marriage. The marriage we both knew was ordained by God!

> *Be alert and of sober mind. Your enemy the devil prowls around like a roaring lion looking for someone to devour*
> *1 Peter 5:8*

The platonic friendship went from a friendly conversations to weekly conversations. I felt strong and unyielding. I was able to share my pain and disappointment with my friend. Besides, he too was a man of God. Needless to say, I felt heard and safe.

I truly felt healed from the betrayal. It was not my intentions to have a serious relationship. But, the enemy began to remind me of the betrayal. Leading me to believe my platonic friend was just someone I could confide in. We went from him talking me through my disappointment to planning a lunch date. Everything inside of me knew that this was not pleasing to God. Again, I heard my Spirit cry out vengeance is mine saith, the Lord, I will repay. What was happening here? Was I giving a deaf ear to God? I was trying to meet a spiritual need (soothing my soul from hurt and disappointment) in a fleshly way. I heard someone say that anger is an emotional punishment you give yourself for somebody else's behavior. Was I punishing my husband or myself? He was already punished.

> But whoso committeth adultery with a woman lacketh understanding: He that doeth it destroyeth his own soul." Proverbs 6:32

Many times I thought I had forgiven him, but I was so angry and disappointed that a part of me wanted to see his downfall. If you've been there then you know what I'm saying. Yet the love I held for him did not allow me to uncover him or bring him to shame. I kept questioning his love for me. My thoughts were all over the place. I thought to myself "Is this man of God he portrays in church and in public a fake? Is he really saved, you know a man after God's own heart. It's no way you can truly love someone and hurt them so deeply, Did he even think of me?"

I did not care that he had apologized a thousand times and tried so hard to do everything to make it up to me. He walked around sad and in fear of losing his marriage. He even told my best friend of 35 years that his family was his life and a divorce (of which I mentioned to him) would destroy him. Still, I wanted God to show his wrath towards him. Maybe his apologies were mirror rehearsed. I kept thinking that if I forgave him it would open the doors for a next time.

Revenge had been planted deeply in my heart. I felt it necessary to get even. Then maybe he would think twice before betraying me again. I was convinced that he would feel my wrath. I was accepting emotional punishment for my husband's behavior.

I accepted a lunch date and a meeting place. I felt spiritually tapped out. I showed up early. We laughed and shared small talk. Nothing happened. It was an innocent lunch date, I told myself. Surely he shared lunch with Lady. Surely they had phone conversations. No way it was a one night stand. Something inspired him to leave the letter!

Needless to say, another lunch date was planned. My thoughts were scattered, yet I heard, walked in the spirit, and you will not fulfill the lust of the flesh. My heart was palpitating. Warning signs were there. I was standing on the corner taking in fresh air and feeling the sun. I was thinking of the smell of his cologne. Suddenly, fear came over me or was it conviction. My anxiety kicked in as I waited for my platonic friend.

In the mist of my waiting, I heard an audible voice whisper, Loveth thou me? I heard the voice loud and clearly. So clear that I whispered emotionally and I believed internally, Yes Lord! Tears began to flood my eyes. I began looking around to see if anyone was paying attention. Then I heard the same voice ask, "Who do you love the most?" This can't be happening. Not here, not now. I took off like a Russian mighty wind. I abandoned the mission and speed walked back to my car. When I made it to my car, I was trembling uncontrollably. I was crying loudly. I kept saying , you Lord, you... I love you the most.

> "For this thing I besought the Lord thrice, that it might depart from me. And he said unto me, My grace is sufficient for thee: for my strength is made perfect in weakness. Most gladly therefore will I rather glory in my infirmities, that the power of Christ may rest upon me. Therefore I take pleasure infirmities, in reproaches, in necessities, in persecutions, in distresses for Christ's sake: for when I am weak, then am I strong." 2 Corinthians 12:8-10 KJV

I thought I knew myself better. I thought I was strong enough. At least the enemy tried to convince me that I was. I was so disappointed in myself. How did I allow this to go so far? What a foolish woman. The same woman who preached with confidence. Nothing shall be able to separate me from the love of God, which is in Christ Jesus. I said nothing. Why was I there? I hurriedly drove home. I could not return to work.

I made it home safely thanks to almighty God. I remember falling to my knees, again, I was crying uncontrollably. I remember saying, God it hurts so much! The answer in a question form was life changing.

Do you remember the time you intentionally left that lipstick stained napkin. God brought it back to my memory like it was yesterday. Imagine how she must have felt. I begin sobbing and sobbing. I immediately started repenting begging for Mercy. I would never want to cause anyone this type of anger, pain and hurt. I started praying for the woman's marriage I had violated. My heart was overwhelmed with sorrow. The lipsticked napkin was many years before my marriage. Now, the sealed letter my husband had written to Lady. The struggle to forgive was over. I understood. I was reaping what I had sown. Wow! Just wow I thought. God is not a man that He should lie.

A man reaps what he sows. Whoever sows to please their flesh, from the flesh will reap destruction; whoever sows to please the Spirit, from the Spirit will reap eternal life. Let us not become weary in doing good, for at the proper time we will reap a harvest if we do not give up" (Galatians 6:7–9).

Do not be deceived: God cannot be mocked. A man reaps what he sows. Whoever sows to please their flesh, from the flesh will reap destruction; whoever sows to please the Spirit, from the Spirit will reap eternal life. Let us not become weary in doing good, for at the proper time we will reap a harvest if we do not give up.

Galations 6:7-9

What's next I thought? Without hesitation, forgiveness was the first thing on my list. "For if ye forgive men their trespasses, your heavenly Father will also forgive you: but if ye forgive not men their trespasses, neither will your Father forgive your trespasses." Matthew 6:14-15 KJV.

I was ever so ready to forgive!!!

All things work together for good to them that love God, to them who are the called according to his purpose. Romans 8:28.

For if you forgive other people when they sin against you, your heavenly Father will also forgive you. But if you do not forgive others their sins, your Father will not forgive your sins.
Matthew 6:14-15

And we know that in all things God works for the good of those who love him, who[a] have been called according to his purpose.
Romans 8:28

Chapter 5

Trust Issues

I read a quote somewhere that stated, Don't let yesterday's fight stop today's communication. I believed I had forgiven him for the betrayal. No more battling with the why and how did it happen. Everybody deserves a second chance, even me.

I loved him. I wanted to make it work, but can I trust him again? How do you separate trust and respect? Can I not trust him, but still respect him? I found it extremely hard trying to respect someone I had trust issues with. What if there is more than just one other woman? What if there are multiple women? Multiple women would be better right? Then maybe he's just in midlife crisis and not seriously attached to Lady.

Wait, I know, I know I said he was forgiven. It's not like I wanted to continue dwelling on the past. It's just that it popped up in my mind sometimes. Out of no where, it just popped up. At times I could shake it, other times I couldn't. Well like mother said, "you can't erase the past." I realized that forgiving doesn't lead to forgetting. I believe we have to just forgive every time we remember the hurt. I couldn't replace the pain with a better image in my mind. Sometimes that can be bad too. Because the new image wasn't him.

There's something strange about me and my thought process in a serious relationship. It's like this. If you don't love me. I don't love you either. It ain't a one way street. I am not chasing after you. If I love you, I love you, but you have to love me back. If the love is not reciprocated, Im done. And also, You can't love two of us. He said I was the one. The wife he prayed for. The wife he brought home to his grandparents for a final stamp of approval. They even gave him the GO! His actions were not matching his words. How can I trust that again? Wait... Im rambling again. All that's behind me. He showed me what he was capable of doing while supposedly being in love with me. But, anyways, I'm good. I turned him over to Jesus. Like mom would say, "That's between him and the God he serves." Another question is, can I be trusted?

I downplayed my part in the betrayal.

I was sitting home being a good wife and mother. A good steward! I was active in ministry, yet nothing came before my family. My family was my life. I had surrendered my life to Jesus a long time ago. I was wrapped up, tied up and tangled up in Jesus.I was so much at peace.

I wanted to believe that my husband was the reason I backslid! He provoked me to anger! I read it in the Bible. "Provoke not…….to wrath" or something like that. Ugh. I kept thinking I had forgiven my spouse, but I didn't. Not only did I not forgive him, I no longer trusted him. I blamed him! I know I sound confused. I am. I mean I was. I don't know right now. You can feel delusional sometimes after you experience infidelity. It's been years, but even writing this book triggered me. I wrote/ write in past and present voices. God ushers me back to safety. Back to the book.

I don't think I have forgiven myself. I believed I had. I mean I had trust issues. I spent so much time trying to find blame. Blaming him for starting this betrayal journey and me for finishing it. I think in the beginning I did believe that all men cheated. I should have expected it. Yet, It was my fairytale heart that thought differently.

After all of this drama, forgiveness was not the big problem. The problem was trusting again. It was complicated moving forward, not being able to trust him or myself. I was forewarned about trusting men. I knew that women could not be trusted. Eve proved that in the garden. Adam proved to be easily persuaded. I thought I had been delivered from that wickedness. I saw myself differently. Trustworthy was my middle name. Truth is, once you are betrayed it shifts how you show up in a relationship.

Chance Marshall MA, HCPC, writes: Trust from both partners are the pillars that hold up a relationship, and when they're knocked, disconnection occurs. When you can no longer be vulnerable with the other person, you begin to experience different things in your relationship. Chance is a founding partner & the BADth (British Association of Dramatherapists) Lead therapist at Self Space and Head of Written and Digital Content.

How do you continue to show up faithful and trusting in a marriage after betrayal? The broken trust? The deceit? The lies? The feeling of hate?!

I was so disappointed in myself. I wish I would have been more concerned with pleasing God when I was broken. I wish I could go back and clean it up, but I cannot. Why couldn't I shake these trust issues?

I felt prepared to take on any evil attack on our marriage. I preached a sermon to a Church full of souls. Again on forgiveness. I stood firmly on the 70 times 7 forgiveness stance. I said nothing my husband could do would change who I was. I stated that I had 70 times 7 , plus some forgiveness for him.

I wasn't expecting adultery to be one of those needing to be forgiven. And I felt positive that I would not show up in that lineup. Not even attempted adultery.

Never say never. I couldn't be trusted either.

My husband was not responsible for my response. That was a weak way out. I was unfaithful to my true love. The one who always had me covered. The most faithful love I have ever known. He called me friend. He even laid down His life for me. There is no greater love than this. My love for God is personal. It's not based on some sinner man saved by grace. If you betray me, I betray God. That's insane right? I didn't really have trust issues with God. I had trust issues with both me and my husband. Can God count on me to be faithful again?

Scriptures are all good when we are throwing them at other people. I said throwing, because sometimes we can be insensitive when dealing with the pain of others. Especially if we are feeling safe in our marriage. Keep your eyes on God we tell them. Nothing should be able to separate you from His love. Don't let another person's actions take your eyes off of God. Keep your head up. And above all, remain faithful! Until we walk a mile or a block in someone else's shoes. We can't ever trust ourselves. Trust issues are inevitable. Psalms 118:8 states that it is better to trust in the LORD than to put confidence in man.

> *It is better to trust in the Lord than to put confidence in man.*
> *Psalms 118:8*

We often state that if I had known in the beginning what I know right now, my marriage would have been a lot different. Well for me, all the knowledge in the world could not have prepared me for this complex season of marriage. The longer you do life, the more you understand your need for God!

My husband not being trustworthy was one thing. The irony of my trustworthiness left me in despair. So… I can't be trusted either. That was really big for me. I too became a part of the trust issues in our marriage. I learned a valuable lesson. I will NEVER give that much power to my husband or any human being. I felt annoyed at the thought of the expectations of him I held. But, can you imagine the disgust I felt when I didn't meet my own expectations? I thought I had arrived! How can we build this pillar of trust again? As for me, I stopped looking to find love and trust in him, but becoming the love and trust through God in me.

I process marriage very differently now. I am not responsible for my husband's part. I am only responsible for walking as the righteous helpmate he needs. I left the trust issues at the foot of the cross.

God called me! He chose me to be my husband's helpmate. He entrusted him to me. He knew my husband when he was in his mother's womb. God is the only one who has a divine plan for his life. Our husbands are responsible for their purpose. Yes, there should be boundaries in place in marriages.

Yet, it is not our responsibility to micro manage our spouse. Our assignment is to walk by faith, and not by sight. We often respond to what we see and not the ending, which only God foresees. I chose to trust in God not man. I choose to be God's love on display. Two imperfect people trusting a perfect God.

We are on the same team (team Jesus).

My husband is my best friend.

I will never leave my friend in his struggles. I knew who he was in the flesh when I met him. I watched him surrender his life to God. I watched him transition. God knew we would need mercy and grace. Hebrews 4:16 states: Let us therefore come boldly unto the throne of grace, that we may obtain mercy, and find grace to help in time of need."

> *Let us therefore come boldly unto the throne of grace, that we may obtain mercy, and find grace to help in time of need."*
> *Hebrews 4:16*

You can be in the wilderness by design. Matthew 4:1 "Then was Jesus led up of the Spirit into the wilderness to be tempted of the devil."

Why would my husband be exempt? I called it a blessing to be chosen by God. To be a witness that you can make it through the wilderness. Guess what? He made it through too. I feel blessed and highly favored to be his helpmate. What the enemy brought to destroy us, made us stronger and better. We must hold fast to God's word. We must not just read the word, but live the word. "And we know that all things work together for good to those that love God, to those who are the called according to his purpose." Romans 8:28

And we know that all things work together for good to those who love God, to those who are the called according to His purpose
Romans 8:28

Why do christians say, "If you are going to use somebody God, use me."?

Don't answer that question. It was just a thought.

Forgiveness must be on the front line. What about trust?

Maybe we don't have trust issues. Maybe we have purpose issues. God had already made provision for us. I no longer chase answers, ask for explanations or fight for closure.

In a bible plan I studied titled *Courageous and Free, An 8 day Journey to Inner Healing*, Janie Ford, the co-founder of Shelter and Rain wrote, "Are you in a valley of trouble right now? Are you in, or have you been in, a time when you felt alone or isolated? When God leads us through the wilderness, it is so that He can capture our heart. It is there that He speaks tenderly to us and reveals to us who we truly are."

I like to call it "Chosen with purpose." It's when you answer your calling, lean in and trust God!

Chapter 6
Choosing PURPOSE

> *"I press toward the mark for the prize of the high calling of God in Christ Jesus."*
> Philippians 3:14

God's PURPOSE has to be greater than pain and disappointments in marriage. I've chosen purpose over pain. I genuinely forgave my husband and moved on. I no longer desire revenge. I had to first find forgiveness for myself without carrying guilt. Now, I can truly say, I feel healed and not broken. Our bond is stronger than ever. We are partners on a mission to help other couples struggling with infidelity. Is there anything too hard for God? As I mentioned in chapter 4, I had to stop overthinking and revisiting the issues that broke me to pieces and silenced me.

I chose forgiveness and reconciliation.

Our marriage never would have lasted had we not made God a priority and accepted our divine purpose in marriage. Still, it takes time. God's TIME! From the beginning of our marriage… until the end, is a process. In this process were different seasons. Some hard seasons. There were growing and stretching seasons. Amidst God's plan for your marriage is learning your partner and being a helpmate to him as he navigates through life. This can be extremely hard.

During this journey, you could not tell me that what I expected from my Christian husband was not logical, spiritual, and necessary! I read God's word on how a man should love and treat his wife. Surely he read the same thing. Yet, why was he freely deviating from the plan? Why was he making bad choices and multiple mistakes? Choices and mistakes that were not aligned with my agenda. Choices in opposition to God's word. I don't think any of his directives from God included hurt, pain, discontent, disappointment, loneliness, infidelity, etc. right?

I had to continuously remind myself that I was not responsible for how my partner chose to walk. God is omniscience (all knowing). He knew the route my husband would yield to. Scripture was in place for the bad route he chose. And we know that all things work together for good to them that love God, to them who are called according to his purpose, Romans 8:28.

> And we know that God causes everything to work together for the good of those who love God and are called according to his purpose for them
> Romans 8:28

What if my interpretation of a perfect marriage failed to consider these different seasons of life? The hard seasons of marriage. The times that would be spent in the wilderness. GOD had provisions in place for our spouses. He knew that they would need mercy, grace and forgiveness. Proverbs 31:10-12) Forgiving seventy times seventy. Wow! Have we missed the mark.

> A wife of noble character who can find? She is worth far more than rubies. Her husband has full confidence in her
> and lacks nothing of value. She brings him good, not harm,
> all the days of her life.
> Proverbs 31:10-12

My response to his betrayal was humanly painful and I didn't initially choose forgiveness. Choosing forgiveness and reconciliation meant moving forward in alignment with God's purpose. I realized that I had reached a disturbing limit to the 70 times 7 margin of area for my husband.

Forgiveness and departure sound better at that time. To divorce or not to divorce was troubling. Truth is, deep inside I knew I wanted to stay. I knew he needed me. I needed him. We knew we were partnered by God to carry out his divine purpose!

We made a conscious and intentional decision to accept the call.

Beware of the enemy's whispers!

You're just giving him passes to mess up! Do you think God wants you to be a virtuous woman in spite of your husband's unfaithfulness? You should let him know that this is his last mistake. You should put your foot down and demand that he lines up with God's word. Line up or a divorce will be on the table.

You desire to please God. Yet, there are many negative voices working to steal your peace and destroy your purpose!

It's easy to become stagnant, throw in the towel, and get a divorce. We had made it through too many hurdles. I was now in reverse….from flight to fight. I refused to give up. I was confident that he was my life partner. I wanted to see him win. I wanted to see us win. Proverbs 16:9 – The heart of man plans his way, but the Lord establishes his steps. Proverbs 15:22 – Without counsel plans fail, but with many advisers, they succeed. Proverbs 19:21 – Many are the plans in the mind of a man, but it is the purpose of the Lord that will stand.

Yes, the purpose of the Lord did stand!

The heart of man plans his way, but the Lord establishes his steps. Proverbs 16:9

Without counsel plans fail, but with many advisers, they succeed Proverbs 15:22

Many are the plans in the mind of a man, but it is the purpose of the Lord that will stand Proverbs 19:21

Once you've made an until death vow, it's a faith walk through your marriage purpose. Facing infidelity allowed God to refine us. It forced us to acknowledge our true purpose in marriage. We often don't consider a marriage purpose. Sadly, we try to convince ourselves that God would not allow our marriage to go through such trials and tribulations. So some couples jump ship (divorce) and go walk alone. No reason to try to heal something that wasn't ever supposed to be right. Who wants to wait on the Lord and be of good courage walking through infidelity?

We often take the bridle out of God's hand. We try to self control the situation. We want to see immediate, right now changes. Changes according to our time schedule. Again, it takes time. God's time. Not the systematic timeframe of society social norms. Our thought process of once a cheater always a cheater is invalid. That's like saying once you're on drugs, you will die on drugs. Many people are delivered from struggles of many types and never go back. Should we wait for the next time/sin? Was I going to hang on to Moses' written law for divorce? I thought about it, but I chose not to. My husband repented. He was forgiven by God.

To Divorce or Not to Divorce? (Divorce in the Bible: 7 Scripture Verses for Dealing With Divorce, Lindsay Emerson, MA, LMFTA)

So how are we to know if we should seek out divorce, or choose reconciliation? How do we know how to deal with infidelity Biblically in our own, individual situations?

I believe the answer has everything to do with repentance. Look at what God said to Israel after He divorced her:

God was willing to reconcile Himself to Israel if she would only repent and turn back to Him. If we want to know how to deal with infidelity Biblically, I believe we'll do the same.

Yes, to reconcile after infidelity is an act of grace, but our God lavishes grace upon us every day, and as His people, we are called to live gracious lives.

If there is true, genuine, and complete repentance on the part of the betrayer, God can restore what has been broken. A new covenant can be made. If, however, there is no repentance, then I believe **1 Corinthians 5** tells us what we must do.

How Can I Know if there is True Repentance?

Of course, we can't see the heart of another, so how can we ever really know if there is repentance or not? How are we supposed to figure out how to deal with infidelity biblically if we can't ever know for sure if we're still being lied to or manipulated?

These are hard questions to answer, but the Bible gives us some pretty great advice on the matter. The first thing we need to understand is that while we can't see anyone else's heart, God can. He not only knows what is going on in our spouse's heart right now, but He knows what was going on in there yesterday, and what will be going on in there tomorrow.

We can trust Him to lead us into all truth.

God promises that if we need wisdom on any matter, we need only ask, and He will help us. (James 1:5-8)

> *If any of you lacks wisdom, you should ask God, who gives generously to all without finding fault, and it will be given to you. But when you ask, you must believe and not doubt, because the one who doubts is like a wave of the sea, blown and tossed by the wind. That person should not expect to receive anything from the Lord. Such a person is double-minded and unstable in all they do*
> *James 1: 5-8*

The Bible also teaches us that we're not supposed to depend on our own understanding of any situation, but to trust in the Lord with all our heart, acknowledge Him in everything we do, and wait for Him to show us which path to take. (Proverbs 3:5-6)

> *Trust in the Lord with all your heart and lean not on your own understanding;*
> *in all your ways submit to him, and he will make your paths straight.*
> *Proverbs 3: 5-6*

Finally, we find in Scripture that there is something called Fruits of the Spirit. These are measurable by-products of a Holy-Spirit filled life. The fruits of the Spirit includes things like love, joy, peace, patience, kindness, goodness, faithfulness, gentleness, and self-control, and stands in sharp contrast to the fruit of the flesh. (Galatians 5)

> *But the fruit of the Spirit is love, joy, peace, forbearance, kindness, goodness, faithfulness, gentleness and self-control. Against such things there is no law. Those who belong to Christ Jesus have crucified the flesh with its passions and desires. Since we live by the Spirit, let us keep in step with the Spirit. Let us not become conceited, provoking and envying each other.*
> *Galatians 5:22-26*

In an online article by Broken Vows Restored, the author discusses how a person who has humbled himself before God in repentance will live a life which bears out the fruit of the Spirit. It cannot be faked, not consistently or for any significant length of time anyhow. If we see within the life of our spouse the consistent fruit of the flesh, it is unlikely that repentance has taken place. If, however, we see love, joy, peace, patience, kindness, goodness, faithfulness, gentleness, and self-control becoming a bigger and bigger part of his life, we can trust that this is a result of the active work of the Holy Spirit, and it only happens in a repentant heart.

In marriage/partnership, development and growth takes time. God's time. I made a commitment to God to be a help mate. I promised to love and honor through sickness and health, good and bad, for as long as we both shall live.

I was trusting God to restore my marriage. I was willing to forgive and move on. I had to remember that I am responsible for my calling and purpose as a help mate. We cannot control our husband's part in the marriage. We can set boundaries in our new journey towards recovery, with mutual love and respect.

A Godly marriage is God's love on display.

It's a faith walk. The reality is, many marriages aren't on display on purpose. I do not accept the notion that a one- sided relationship cannot work. Clinical psychologist Scott Bea explains that a one-sided relationship has more uncertainty. He states that it boils down to one person doing more heavy lifting; emotionally, physically or mentally. A relationship where it feels like the effort, energy and task are imbalanced. Unlike a friendship, a partnership one-sided relationship is more penalizing.

When you grow in wisdom and knowledge you understand a one-sided relationship differently. The relationship is not a 50-50 thing. One day you may share a 50-50 load. Another day could be an 80-20 load. It is no longer seen as one-sided, but rather a team effort to complete the task. The strong baring the infirmities of the weak.

I have embraced my purpose as a help mate.….a virtuous woman!

Help as a verb:
make it easier for (someone) to do something by offering one's services or resources.

Help as a noun;
the action of helping someone to do something; assistance .

  Help mate? My first thought as I shared in the 1st chapter was to throw the whole husband away. The pain was so deep and particularly disheartening. Mainly, because I felt it could've been prevented.

  Did he just runoff one day and sleep with a stranger? Was it a relationship of intimacy? Was it someone I knew?

  Do you know what it feels like walking around staring at random women wondering could that be her. Even in your circle you're staring, because you've lost all trust. A part of you wants to shrink, just disappear. You want to hide from the stares, which probably were not stares just my insecurities.

Early on I shared how hard it would be to trust my husband again. I just wanted him to fall off of a cliff or to be stuck under the bottom of a ship. If you've been there you know there were days that you repent all day long. God please forgive my thoughts and strengthen my heart. Father hold me in your bosom. Hide me in the secret of your tabernacle.

Then you remember the assignment, your purpose, commitment, accountability and consistency to reconcile. You put on the armor of God. You embody this helpmate empowered by God. You remember your vow to love through good or bad until death do you part. Oh wait, does this mean that bad could possibly include hurt, pain, disappointment, discontent, loneliness, infidelity, etc? The answer was a yes for me. This angered me and most likely other women who has experienced some of the same issues of life. The broken covenant. It seems like we are giving them a free ticket to fall short. Well I personally don't think we are. It's not mine or yours to give. If you have chosen reconciliation, prepare for the best.

> *The LORD will give grace and glory: No good thing will he withhold from them that walk uprightly.*
> *Psalm 84:11*

God gives free will and mercy and grace. If a man's free will leads to sin of any kind, even if it's against us, there are consequences from God. It doesn't have to be vengeance from us or divorce. It's your choice!

Psalm 57:2 says, "I cry out to God Most High, to God who fulfills his purpose for me." This is key in understanding God's purpose for your life. God has numbered your days and will fulfill every purpose He has for you.

However, our choices and actions also really matter.

I cry out to God Most High, to God, who vindicates me
Psalms 57:2

Chapter 7
Surviving Infidelity

> *"But whoso committeth adultery with a woman lacketh understanding: He that doeth it destroyeth his own soul."*
> *Proverbs 6:32*

"True love can survive the strongest and most painful of times", *Pastor T.D. Jake's, The Potter's House.* We are now and have always been life partners ordained by God! Even knowing with all my heart that God joined us together, I wanted to opt out. The struggle to overcome infidelity was destructive and a PAIN that is inevitable. This was a pivotal moment in my life. The survival wasn't easy, but it was worth it.

> *"But Jesus beheld them, and said unto them, With men this is impossible; but with God all things are possible."*
> *Matthew 19:26*

> *"For I am persuaded, that neither death, nor life, nor angels, nor principalities, nor powers, nor things present, nor things to come, nor height, nor depth, nor any other creature, shall be able to separate us from the love of God, which is in Christ Jesus our Lord."*
> *Romans 8:38-39*

I was reminded more than ever before the urgency to live out loud the scriptures that are hidden on the table of our hearts. I was challenged to forgive and extend true unconditional love in the mist of pain, distress, discomfort and disappointment. Andy Stanley, the founder and senior pastor of North Point Ministries, stated that there is no such thing as deep teaching when it comes to Christ.....only deep living. It was deep living in God's word for me. It was a real renewing of the mind thing.

Simply stated, renewing my mind according to Romans 12:2 meant interpreting life through the lens of God's Word and the inspiration of the Holy Spirit, rather than through the lens of my experience, wounds, trauma, preferences, or the opinions of others.

> And be not conformed to this world: but be ye transformed by the renewing of your mind, that ye may prove what is that good, and acceptable, and perfect, will of God.
> Romans 2:12

We spend so much time contemplating how we will respond to sin. The sins we disapprove of. You know the unforgivable ones. The one's we are most embarrassed by. The one that folks tend to call you weak for forgiving. The ones that don't deserve forgiveness in the earthly eyes of man. The ones that brought hurt, pain, disappointment, discontent, loneliness like infidelity. Especially infidelity. The sin that God forgave David of (with consequences.). David went as far as having Bathsheba's husband killed. Yet he was called a man after God's own heart.

God also forgave Abraham from impregnating his handmaid because of his lack of faith (with consequences). Abraham became known as the father of many nations.

After reading an article online by the family life, I was reminded that if you decide to give your marriage a chance, let it be a bonded relationship that "mirrors" God's sacrificial, unconditional, lasting love for his children (those who by faith have accepted His sacrifice in adoption into his eternal family.)

Our Latter is Truly Greater

We are in another season. We have transitioned into our senior years. The latter is truly greater! I wouldn't trade my friend, my lover, my children's father for nothing in this world. I thank God for choosing me, ordaining me and preparing me for the journey. My husband and I were lead to start a marriage ministry outreach. Our desire is to encourage other couples to surrender their marriage to God. Trust Him and NEVER doubt. Philippians 1:6 "being confident of this very thing, that he which hath begun a good work in you will perform it until the day of Jesus Christ:" Is there anything too hard for God!!!!

> *Being confident of this very thing, that he which hath begun a good work in you will perform it until the day of Jesus Christ:*
> *Philippians 1:6*

Oh what a time we had on our eight day cruise Vacation at Sea, June 2023. We sailed to Aruba, grand Turk and Curacao in 8 days. It was rejuvenating. We desperately needed the "US" time.

Sometimes you have to get away, digress, refocus, and reset. Yes, we are still in love. I will love him until death do us part. Yes, we are a team, team Jesus! We are walking in purpose! We are showing up in marriage "as God's love on display!

NOTE : You must continue to allow space for seasons of transitioning. Who we were in our 20s and 30s are not the same people we are in our 50s - 70s. You are wiser and stronger. Allow each other room and grace to age peacefully as individuals, but on the same team. Support each other as you embark upon new challenges as you grow older. Practice clear communication. Be kind! Be gentle! most importantly, remember, your marriage has purpose, God's purpose. We are looking forward to celebrating our 40th year of marriage with promise, grace, favor and forgiving hearts!

Helpful resources on Surviving Infidelity

What should be the response of a Christian whose spouse has had an affair?

BE FORGIVEN. "If we confess our sins, he is faithful and just and will forgive us our sins and purify us from all unrighteousness" (1 John 1:9). When a marriage is in crisis, both parties should ask God to help them see how each may have contributed to the whole situation and be released from the weight of guilt before God. From that point on, here will be freedom to seek His counsel and guidance. His Holy Spirit will enable theto do what they could not do on their own. "I can do all this through him who gives me strength" (Philippians 4: 13)

> *If we confess our sins, he is faithful and just to forgive us our sins, and to cleanse us from all unrighteousness.*
> 1 John 1:9

> *I can do all things through Christ which strengtheneth me.*
> Philippians 4:13

As God leads, true forgiveness and reconciliation are possible. No matter how long it takes, every effort must be made to forgive and reconcile (Matthew 5:23–24). As to whether to stay or to leave, "whoever divorces his wife and marries someone else commits adultery—unless his wife has been unfaithful" (Matthew 19:9). While the innocent party may have grounds for divorce, God's preference is forgiveness and reconciliation.

> Therefore if thou bring thy gift to the altar, and there rememberest that thy brother hath ought against thee;
> Leave there thy gift before the altar, and go thy way; first be reconciled to thy brother, and then come and offer thy gift
>
> Matthew 5: 23-24

> And I say unto you, Whosoever shall put away his wife, except it be for fornication, and shall marry another, committeth adultery: and whoso marrieth her which is put away doth commit adultery.
>
> Matthew 19: 9

In summary, when a Christian's spouse has had an affair, the wronged party must guard against bitterness (Hebrews 12:15) and be careful not to repay evil for evil (1 Peter 3:9). We should be willing to forgive and genuinely want reconciliation; at the same time, we should not extend forgiveness to the unrepentant. In all things we must seek the Lord and find our wholeness and healing in Him.

> Not rendering evil for evil, or railing for railing: but contrariwise blessing; knowing that ye are thereunto called, that ye should inherit a blessing.
>
> 1 Peter 3:9

> Looking diligently lest any man fail of the grace of God; lest any root of bitterness springing up trouble you, and thereby many be defiled;
>
> Hebrews 12:15

The Mayo Clinic Staff defines Infidelity as: Mending your marriage after an affair. They state that infidelity may cause intense emotional pain, but an affair doesn't have to mean the end of a marriage. It is imperative to understand how a marriage can be rebuilt after an affair. For many individuals, it is hard to think that a relationship can survive infidelity and part of the healing process involves reflecting on what occurred and why. Most importantly, relationships can survive infidelity when both parties are willing to work together on healing and move forward in the relationship.

Help for Broken Marriages

The damage in the wake of intimate betrayal is great! Marriages lie in ruins and families struggle to remain in tact. But the pain, the shame, the broken trust – it can all be redeemed! We serve the God who makes beauty from ashes. He's in the business of restoring broken marriages! When we surrender our mess to Him, He'll make a pathway through the wilderness and create rivers of living water in the dry wasteland.

> *But forget all that – it is nothing compared to what I am going to do. For I am about to do something new. See, I have already begun! Do you not see it? I will make a pathway through the wilderness. I will create rivers in the dry wasteland.*
>
> *Isaiah 43:18-19*

A Beautiful Story That Proves Marriage Can Survive An Affair

Testimony by: Cherith Peters

I am a wife, mother, and passionate follower of my Lord and Savior, Jesus Christ. After the realities of my husband's infidelity finally came to a head, I began blogging about our journey to healing. God has worked many miracles in our life and marriage since then, and grown a ministry committed to helping others find the healing in Christ that changed our story forever!

@hisdearlyloveddaughter

https://www.instagram.com/hisdearlyloveddaughter/

Cherith is just one of the many women who have chosen to forgive and have been given beauty for ashes. It is helpful and encouraging to talk with others who have experienced similiar pain. Joining a group or simply reading about others journeys can aide you in your healing process.

> To appoint unto them that mourn in Zion, to give unto them beauty for ashes, the oil of joy for mourning, the garment of praise for the spirit of heaviness, that they might be called trees of righteousness, the planting of the Lord, that He might be glorified.
> Isaiah 61:3

Chapter 8

I Am Keeping My Husband!

I'm keeping him. I mean my life partner and children's father. Yall when I said yes to my husband, I didn't know if he was the one. He said to me on our first date, a woman like you I can spoil to death. I didn't know how to respond to such flattery. I was a single mother. I had two sons out of wedlock; Two precious sons who simply adored me. Still, I had made a mess of my life.

I was the product of a father with a 7th grade education and a mother with a 3rd grade education. My father was incarcerated, because under the influence of alcohol he took the life of his best friend. He also would beat my mother until she was unrecognizable. I watched it like a scary movie on television. It caused me to have anxiety and a nervous disorder. My mom was heavy on the bottle. She was trying to survive domestic violence. We lived daily with the expectation that after his release he would return and kill his entire family (It's what he said to us). He said if he could not have us no one else could.

Prior to marrying my mother, he was a World War II veteran who was captured and made prisoner of war. He came home mentally damaged. I got the damaged version of him. He went to prison when I was 12 years old. I received the best version of my mother that she could possible give.

   Early on in life even before having kids, I made a decision that I would be a top notch mom. I promised that I would NEVER expose my children to the toxic behaviors that I was exposed to. Without proper direction, life happened and I had two sons. One day I realized that life was no longer about me, but about my children. I needed them to have the best life that little boys could have. So, I enrolled in business school. I graduated and landed a decent job at city hall under the leadership of Mayor Ernest "Dutch" Morial. I was a proud somebody. Initially, I was settling for whatever man would pick me. I didn't feel like I was in a position to have options.

   Finally, I was feeling good about myself and where I was going. I then felt as if I had something to bring to the table. Perhaps now I have options. It was me and my boys living a comfortable and productive life. My eldest was in a magnet school and my youngest was in a college prep preschool academy. I had given them stability.

When I met my husband, he approached me with confidence and certainty. He included my sons in his conversations. He said those boys need a father. I told him that their father was JESUS! At that time I was practicing celibacy. I made a conscious decision to put my life on hold and consider what my sons needed. They needed a father. When you have children out of wedlock it can be very scary, especially without parental guidance. Nevertheless, I felt the need to sacrifice any desires or needs that I thought I had for the sake of my sons.

I had surrendered my life to God. I was not a bible scholar, but I believed in his existence. I watched my mother kneel in prayer and have conversations with Him. I heard her ask for protection and freedom from the bondage of my father. God did just that. So in my little world and prayer life I would ask God for a father for my children. I would say "God I will know he is the one if he does not ask me for SEX." A husband that will provide and protect us. I promised you that was my simple little prayer request. I did not know that the man who said I was the one knew what he was talking about. Yet, he seemed convinced and he moved with action. Believe it or not he did not ask me for sex.....NEVER doing our dating period.

I can tell you, God is bigger than anything I've seen. God met me right where I was. He knew I was depending on him to guide and protect me and my kids. He was the only one I trusted. My little BIG faith trusted Him without doubt. So when my now husband did not ask for sex and continued to pursue me and respect me, my heart opened. I was convinced in my little world that God had answered my prayers.

Again, God met me where I was. I want to think that my little faith moved God. Forty years later, we have raised 11+ children who are productive citizens in society. My husband has always been a provider and protector. He continues to provide and protect. He has been my constant friend. My life partner. He took on a woman and two children and all the damage/baggage that came with me.

Years later I asked my husband a question. Dear why are you still here? We have been a pretty good team. I said, "The children are grown and I am still a bit insane to say the least. His answer was simple, "God told me to marry you and to take care of you. I no longer question God. No matter the task. I suit up and give it my best shot." I am getting a little emotional writing this. To be honest, I was looking for a mushie, lovey dovey answer. You know like...you're all that and a bag of chips, but I didn't get that. Nothing my husband said was about me, but all about God.

I wasn't called to be his foxy mama or arm candy, but a helpmate. One that would help him navigate as we said yes to this partnership. It wasn't a fairytale marriage reality. It was ministry! It was purposed! And you know what, I happily accepted my husband's answer. I'm happy that God chose to use me as a vessel. I also took accountability for my immature decisions.

God took the mess that I had made and turned it into something good. "And we know that all things work together for good to them that love God, to them who are the called according to his purpose." Romans 8:28

> *And we know that all things work together for good to those who love God, to those who are the called according to His purpose.*
>
> *Romans 8:28*

My advice to any woman, especially those with children; HEAL before you add to your trauma. You don't have to look for a husband, he will find you. You are already a good thing and in finding you, your husband will obtain favor from the Lord.

In conclusion, I'm not throwing my husband away. I'm not throwing away the man that God sent. A marriage that God sealed for His purpose. God predestined this marriage to be so. This marriage is not about my husband's infidelity, but rather purposed unto GOD for His glory. I have ever desired to continue a God centered marriage. Yet, I'm not the young immature woman that I use to be. Total investment in our marriage on the same accord is mandatory.....no other way!

In an online devotional by ligonier.org, they state that, "God must be first in marriage for it to be lived to his glory, on display!"

Marriage is secondary and temporary, and God is primary and infinite.

I present my marriage to you as "God's love on display!!! Purpose over Pain.

-Romella

About The Author

Romella Hodges, a proud native of New Orleans, embodies the spirit of her city with a heart full of love, community, and service. A wife of 40 years, Romella has been blessed with over 10 children and has dedicated her life to nurturing not only her own family but also those in need. She holds both a bachelor's in sociology and a master's degree in liberal arts from Tulane University and has served as a ministry leader for more than 30 years.

Driven by her passion for helping others, Romella founded a nonprofit organization focused on underserved teens, later becoming a foster parent herself. She has also traveled the world teaching and training others in the art of evangelism, a mission she continues today. Her lifelong dedication to service and learning has continued into her latter years, where she now serves as the lead advisor for each of her children's businesses.

Romella is often described as a "mother to the motherless" and a true Proverbs 31 woman. She is a friend to all she meets, a testament to God's grace, and a beacon of love and strength. Her life is a reflection of the rich culture and enduring sense of togetherness that New Orleans is known for, and her legacy of faith, family, and community continues to inspire all who cross her path.

'Remember always, that you are God's love on display"
-Romella Hodges

Made in the USA
Columbia, SC
02 November 2024